Original title:
The Banana's Song

Copyright © 2025 Creative Arts Management OÜ
All rights reserved.

Author: Evan Hawthorne
ISBN HARDBACK: 978-1-80586-269-7
ISBN PAPERBACK: 978-1-80586-741-8

Carnival of Colors in the Orchard

In the orchard where fruits play,
Bouncing colors bright and gay,
Lemons wear a sunny grin,
While cherries dance in their skin.

Peaches puff in rosy tune,
Grapes giggle 'neath the moon,
Twirling in the gentle breeze,
Tickled by the swaying trees.

Oranges roll with joyful cheer,
Mangoes hum, they're full of beer,
Bananas wearing silly hats,
Chiming in with silly chats.

Here in this delightful scene,
Fruits unite, a jolly team,
In the carnival of delight,
Every color shines so bright.

Sounds of the Sunshine Serenade

The sun awakes with playful rays,
As fruits all gather for their plays,
A symphony of peels and rinds,
Echoing through the leafy binds.

Pineapple strums a golden tune,
While papayas groove in afternoon,
Fruits frolic on the lawn today,
In a serenade of bright bouquet.

With zest they sing, from high to low,
Guava twirls, bananas go,
Each one adds their own sweet spin,
Making music, letting in.

Laughter swirls in every note,
Jellybeans, watch them float,
In this orchard's sunny glow,
Where joy and rhythm freely flow.

Tropical Whispers

Whispers dance among the trees,
Tropical tales on the breeze,
Mangoes tell of summer nights,
While coconuts share sweet delights.

The playful wind hums a song,
Carrying laughter all along,
Bananas chuckle in sweet glee,
While shadows play hide and seek.

Pineapples sway in the sun,
Every fruit joins in the fun,
Watermelons laugh so loud,
Bouncing like a jolly crowd.

In the dance, all troubles flee,
Tropical vibes, wild and free,
Each note carries a blissful tune,
Underneath the watchful moon.

Golden Melodies

Golden fruits in vivid sight,
Swaying softly, pure delight,
Fruits in harmony, they play,
Singing songs of bright array.

Lemons laugh like little kids,
Apricots. Oh, how they hid,
Under leaves so bright and green,
Where the sun's a friendly sheen.

Lush and sunny, every slice,
Creates a melody so nice,
Bananas giggle with a grin,
Playing tunes that draw you in.

In this orchard, joy abounds,
With each note, a new joy found,
Golden melodies fill the air,
A fruity fest beyond compare.

Harvesting Joy in Rhythm

In the grove, laughter rings,
Chasing tails, and silly swings,
With every peel, a giggle flies,
As bright as the sun in endless skies.

Tropical breezes dance along,
Fruitful cheers, a merry song,
In playful jumps, we sway and spin,
Harvesting joy, let the fun begin!

The Bliss Found in Yellow

Golden globes sway with glee,
Life's a party, can't you see?
With each bite, a chuckle blooms,
Brightening up the dullest rooms.

Peeling laughter, tangy delight,
Chasing dreams through day and night,
Creamy treats in a playful dance,
Join the fun, just take a chance!

Melody Under the Sunlit Canopy

Under leaves, a tune we find,
Nature's groove, free and kind,
Twists and turns, our hearts align,
With every moment, smiles entwine.

Dancing shadows, laughter flows,
Like a river, humor grows,
Let the rhythm take you far,
Together we'll shine, a dazzling star!

Nature's Sweetest Echo

Echoes bounce in vibrant cheer,
From the grove, we'll draw near,
With every pluck, a burst of fun,
Life's sweetest joys for everyone.

Breezy whispers tease the play,
Waving worries far away,
In fruity laughter, we find our role,
Harvesting sunshine for every soul!

Vibrations of Golden Light

In a grove where laughter grows,
Fruits converse in silly prose.
Peeling jokes with zest and cheer,
Golden bites will draw you near.

Bouncing high on sunny rays,
Making up the silliest plays.
Nature's giggles fill the air,
Joyful scents beyond compare.

With each twist and playful grin,
A treasure hunt for sweetest skin.
Silly shadows dance around,
In this place, pure fun is found.

Swirling in the Sunset Glow

Underneath the twinkling skies,
Fruity fun, a sweet surprise.
Dancing leaves with jolly glee,
Whispering secrets of the tree.

Clouds burst forth in giggly hue,
With every turn, there's something new.
Twisting and spinning, we all go,
Swirling round in sunset's show.

The day drifts by with laughter loud,
Nature's joy, the playful crowd.
Snickering fruits on every branch,
In the twilight, let's all dance.

Blissful Note of Nature's Bounty

In a place where wonders sprout,
Silly songs and laughs throughout.
Nature strums a jolly tune,
Bouncing berries make them swoon.

A laugh from leaves, a giggle bright,
Fruits in sync, a pure delight.
Harmony under the blue dome,
With every melody, we roam.

Chasing dreams on bouncy trails,
Echoing through the happy gales.
Blissful notes, they float on high,
Playful whispers in the sky.

Harvest Moon's Gentle Tune

Underneath the harvest moon,
Fruits break out their happy tune.
With every pluck, a giggle shared,
In the field where joy is bared.

Dancing shadows, bright and spry,
Nature winks as we pass by.
Moonlit fun, a sweet parade,
Golden smiles that never fade.

A joyful crunch with every bite,
Stars above twinkle with delight.
In this harvest, hearts will bloom,
Every fruit sings sweetly, too.

Serenade of the Sunlit Fruit

In a sunny patch, they sway with glee,
Bright and yellow, as happy as can be.
They giggle and wiggle, oh such a sight,
Dancing with joy in the warm daylight.

With every twist, they tease the breeze,
Hanging and swinging, they aim to please.
A group of jesters, they chuckle and laugh,
Creating sweet chaos, a fruity half-craft.

When Gold Meets Green

In a jungle bright where colors blend,
Golden delights on leafy trends.
The air is thick with playful cheer,
As the vibrant fruit whispers, 'Come near!'

With every peel, a giggling burst,
Tropical treasures, a joyful thirst.
Their playful pranks bring smiles to the crowd,
Underneath the trees, they sing out loud.

Laughter in a Tropical Garden

In a garden lush where laughter springs,
Fruitful antics on chatter's wings.
With a crooked smile and a sweet allure,
They jest around like a playful tour.

Tickling leaves, a jolly spree,
Jumps and tumbles, as fun as can be.
With every squish, they make us giggle,
In nature's laughter, we all wiggle.

Caress of the Swinging Branches

Branches twist, in a playful embrace,
Fruits dangle down, full of grace.
A lively chatter, the fruits all share,
As breezes tickle without a care.

Swinging in time, with nature's glee,
Joyful whispers of fruity jubilee.
With every sway, they crack a joke,
In a sunlit world, they happily poke.

Refuge of the Ripe

In a land where laughter grows,
A fruity friend, everyone knows.
Swinging high, a yellow delight,
Bringing smiles, morning and night.

Peeling layers of joy so sweet,
A silly dance, with wiggly feet.
Bouncing up, just like a cheer,
Who could frown when fun is near?

Walking Under Yellow Canopies

Underneath the sunny hue,
Giggles sprout like morning dew.
Every step, a playful jig,
Dancing under the bright and big.

Laughter blooms with every sway,
Poking fun, come what may.
In a world that's bright and bold,
Silly tales begin to unfold.

The Colorful Song of Laughter

A chorus of giggles fills the air,
As yellow friends sway without a care.
Every note, a burst of cheer,
Ring out loud for all to hear.

Harmony in every peel,
Making life a grand big deal.
Funny faces, jolly sight,
Creating joy, pure delight.

Temptation From Above

Hanging high, a juicy tease,
Whispers sweet on the warm breeze.
Fingers reach for yellow dreams,
Laughter echoes, bursting seams.

A playful pluck, a teasing game,
Who can resist? It's never the same.
With a wiggle and a smile so wide,
A fruit can bring joy, what a ride!

The Sweet Symphony of Growth

In the sun, yellow smiles play,
Swinging gently, day by day.
Leaves rustle, laughter fills the air,
Nature's dance, without a care.

Sprouting green, then turning gold,
Tales of sweetness waiting to be told.
With each twist, a silly jig,
A fruity tune, not too big.

Bouncing round, the bunches sway,
With the breeze, they laugh and play.
A harmony of silly sights,
Underneath those joyful lights.

Growing tall, they start to sing,
A catchy tune that makes you swing.
With every beat, they spin and whirl,
In a fruity, frollicking swirl.

Dancin' in the Orchard

In the orchard, laughter flows,
Bouncing fruits in bright pink clothes.
Peeling back the layers wide,
Giggling fruits, they just can't hide.

Twisting, turning, round they go,
The merry bunch puts on quite a show.
Under trees where shadows dance,
A joyful jig, a fruit-filled trance.

With every step, a soft thump sound,
Fruit-on-fruit, the joy is found.
Bouncing here, and bouncing there,
In this orchard, fun's everywhere.

Swinging gently, like a breeze,
Fruitful laughter, sure to please.
With every jig and silly move,
In this orchard, we all groove.

Fruitful Harmonies

Under skies of sunny cheer,
Fruits unite, their voices clear.
Swaying hands and wiggly toes,
What a sight, as laughter grows.

Peeling layers, silly skins,
Fluttering hearts, where joy begins.
In fruity choirs, songs arise,
Fruitful melodies touch the skies.

Round and round, in joyful spins,
Amongst the leaves, the laughter wins.
Grapes and apples join the crew,
For musical fun, a lovely view.

With each note, a burst of glee,
Harmonies of us, wild and free.
In a world of citrus cheer,
Singing bright, we persevere.

The Golden Call of the Wild

In the wild, where laughter roams,
Golden fruits find playful homes.
Swinging low, they wave hello,
In the sun's warm, golden glow.

With each rustle, giggles start,
Nature's bounty, a fruity heart.
Dancing lightly through the trees,
In the wild, we live with ease.

A chorus sweet, in harmony,
Bouncing fruits sing joyfully.
Golden calls from nature's band,
Celebrating, hand in hand.

With every twist, a joyful cheer,
In the wild, we're all sincere.
Bouncing here, and laughing loud,
In this symphony, we're proud.

Serenade of Curved Delight

In a bunch they sway and dance,
Each one sporting a bright yellow pants.
With laughter, they giggle and tease,
Bringing joy to the green-leafed breeze.

When the sun peeks from behind the clouds,
They shout in glee, forming crowds.
With a slip and a slide, a playful race,
Rolling down hills, oh what a chase!

They sport their peels, quite proudly so,
Creating smiles wherever they go.
In smoothies, they blend, a creamy treat,
Bringing happiness with each bite we eat.

Chasing monkeys, they love a play,
Hiding behind trees, what a funny display.
With every munch, they promise delight,
Curved delights and smiles, oh so bright!

Sweet Harmony in Yellow

In the fruit bowl, a vibrant cheer,
Golden smiles that bring us near.
With a giggle here, and a squeal there,
They sing sweet songs, filling the air.

Plucked from trees, they dance with glee,
Bananas know how fun life can be.
With every sip of a banana shake,
You'll find laughter that just won't break.

In a pirate hat, they take the stage,
Swaying to music, a fruity page.
With friends around, they'll jest and play,
Turning ordinary into a party day!

Sweet melody in fruity rhyme,
Join the fun—it's banana time!
In the sun, they shine so bright,
Creating smiles from morning till night!

Echoes of the Tropics

Amidst the palm trees, a chatter unfolds,
Bananas reflecting stories untold.
Their curved laughter rings through the air,
A tropical symphony, beyond compare.

Coconuts chuckle, as they roll along,
Joining the fun, singing a song.
With monkeys swinging, and joy they spread,
This fruity fiesta keeps us well-fed.

In vibrant markets, they boast their hue,
Stolen glances, as folks pass through.
Peeking from lunch boxes, they wiggle and sway,
Creating moments brightening the day.

In sweet serenades, they find their bliss,
Never shy to lean in for a kiss.
Under the sun, they dance and twine,
Echoes of laughter, so divine!

Rhapsody of Ripeness

Ripeness is bliss, a fruity affair,
Bouncing on counters without a care.
Beneath the peels, their giggles hide,
In every bite, a joy-filled ride.

In land of sunshine, they hum along,
A merry tune, a carefree song.
Peeling back layers, a standup show,
Grab a fork; let the fun flow!

Native to jungles, they sway in the breeze,
Tickling your senses with such sweet ease.
With each savory slice, they fall and play,
Creating smiles both night and day.

In all their glory, they twirl and spin,
Bananas, the jesters, ready to win.
So take a bite and join the fun,
In this rhapsody, we all become one!

Sunshine's Favorite Tune

In a garden bright and cheery,
Dancing fruits are feeling merry.
With a jig and joyful shout,
Laughing loud, they twist about.

Swinging high upon a vine,
Golden smiles, they intertwine.
Every laugh a bouncing cheer,
Spreading joy, they draw us near.

When the breeze begins to play,
Fruity friends have found their way.
With a giggle and a grin,
Swaying softly in the din.

Oh, the sweetness of the jest,
In this fruity, funny fest.
Join the dance, don't be shy,
Let the laughter lift you high.

The Lush Lyric

In the grove where laughter blooms,
Melodies abound in rooms.
With a wiggle and a bounce,
Fruitful tunes make spirits flounce.

Each banana gives a twirl,
Spinning dreams in every swirl.
Bouncing tunes, both bright and bold,
Echo tales of joy untold.

Underneath the sunlit sky,
Fruits take turns to leap and fly.
They frolic high, they frolic low,
Creating rhythm in a show.

Chiming voices, sweet and clear,
Fruity laughter we all cheer.
Join the fun, don't miss your chance,
Let the orchard lead the dance.

A Fruity Fable

Once upon a sunny day,
Fruits gathered round to play.
With their hats and shoes so bright,
They embarked on sheer delight.

Grapes and pears began to sing,
While the apples spun a ring.
Citrus sprites with zest so grand,
Filled the air, a cheery band.

In their midst, a silly pear,
Tripped and flopped without a care.
Laughter echoed through the trees,
Dancing freely in the breeze.

So remember, laugh and sway,
Join the fruits, don't shy away.
In this tale of fruits and fun,
Every heart will come undone.

Revelry in the Orchard

In the orchard, fun begins,
Fruits all gather, wearing grins.
With a jiggle and a hop,
Round they go, they just can't stop.

Lemons twirl with zestful flair,
Mango muses whirled in air.
Pineapple leads with crazy spins,
While the laughter slowly wins.

As they sing of silly tales,
Wind joins in with joyful wails.
Every branch a stage that's set,
Where the fruits have no regret.

So come and revel in the cheer,
Join the fun, let rhythm steer.
In this place where joy's in bloom,
Catch the spirit, consume the room.

Harmonies of the Tropics

In the jungle where shadows play,
Lively fruits dance throughout the day.
Swinging low on a cheerful breeze,
Nature's laughter among the leaves.

Mangoes giggle, coconuts cheer,
Pineapples join with a flair so clear.
Every whimsy steals the scene,
With rhythm bright in shades of green.

Sunlight trickles, joy ignites,
As fruits come out for their silly fights.
Limes toss jokes, oranges tease,
While passion fruits sway with ease.

Under the sun, what a sight,
A fruity fest, pure delight!
Together they strum their silly song,
In tropic tunes where all belong.

Chorus of Sweet Sunshine

Yellow globes in a happy row,
Swaying to the music's flow.
Whispers of sweetness fill the air,
As fruit-friends gather without a care.

Bouncing on branches, gleefully bright,
Bananas dance, oh what a sight!
They twist and twirl with funny grace,
Creating laughter in every space.

Tropical tunes wrap around the trees,
Singing soft under warm sunbeams.
Papayas giggle, and guavas hum,
In this joyous, fruity kingdom.

From morning light to dusk's embrace,
A chorus plays—a happy place.
Frolic and play, let the fun begin,
In this sunny realm where joy won't thin.

Echoes from the Tree Top

Up in the leaves where giggles hide,
A fruity bunch takes a wild ride.
Banana boots, they bounce and glide,
With laughter echoing far and wide.

Treetop whispers between every swing,
Blend of flavors, what joy they bring!
Nature's party, come join the spree,
Fruits in ragged harmony.

Joking jests float through the air,
Lemons chuckle without a care.
Figs and cherries, a raucous crowd,
Together they cheer—oh so loud!

As the sun dips low with a wink,
Fruity pals gather with a drink.
Under moonlight, they sing and play,
Echoes of joy, come what may.

The Dance of Playful Bananas

In a limbo line, bananas sway,
With tiny hats and a grand display.
Jiving to the beat of a bongo's thump,
They wiggle and giggle with every jump.

Verse by verse, they lift the mood,
A fruity crew, so pure and shrewd.
Dressed in smiles from top to toe,
They're ready for the show, oh yes, let's go!

Bouncing bold with a twist and a spin,
Glamorous and silly—they always win.
Coconut claps and papaya spins,
While peaches cheer, this party begins!

As stars peek down from a velvet sky,
Their laughter dances, oh so high!
Join the fun in this vibrant land,
In the dance of joy, hold a friend's hand.

A Peel of Bliss

Underneath the bright sun,
Bananas laugh and have fun.
With a swing and a sway,
They dance the day away.

Golden skin, such a sight,
Chasing shadows, pure delight.
Twisting, turning in the breeze,
Tickling toes with perfect ease.

When the bunch begins to play,
Fruits unite in a silly way.
Rolling down the garden path,
Laughter echoes, what a laugh!

In the bowl, they sit and tease,
With a giggle, they aim to please.
Peel away troubles galore,
Join the fun, who could ask for more?

The Joyful Chorus

Beneath the trees, a party's started,
With fruity jokes, they'll feel light-hearted.
Chanting tunes, the bananas cheer,
In a fruity band, they're all right here.

Swinging from branches, what a sight!
Yellow smiles shining so bright.
Banana split, a tasty lore,
Makes everyone come back for more!

Jumpy jumps and silly slips,
Together they dance and do fun flips.
With each peel, the giggles grow,
Bananas know how to steal the show!

All day long, they joke and prance,
In the fruit bowl, they love to dance.
A chorus of joy, so pure and bright,
With laughter ringing into the night.

Moonlit Fruit Reverie

In the moonlight, the fruits do gleam,
Bananas giggle, living the dream.
Swinging soft on a gentle breeze,
Under starlight, they frolic with ease.

Whispers sweet in fruity tones,
Ticklish laughter and playful groans.
Swaying softly like a ship at sea,
Bananas grinning, wild and free.

A hidden spot where the bright rays play,
As they chat about their sunny day.
Peeled back secrets, no need to hide,
In this moonlit world, we take pride.

They toss silly jokes to the night,
In this reverie, everything's bright.
With a wink and a cheerful cheer,
Fruit friends forever, we hold so dear.

Rhymes of the Rainforest

In the rainforest, where the wild hearts roam,
Bananas sing songs from their leafy home.
With a twist and a turn, they steal the scene,
Bright yellow laughter, of fruit so keen.

Among the creatures, a funny display,
Bananas make jokes in a wobbly ballet.
Hopping and skipping like a fun parade,
No frowns allowed, all worries delayed.

They joke with monkeys, swing so high,
Tickling toads as they leap by.
With a splash in puddles, they giggle and roar,
In this tropical land, they always want more.

Come join the fun, leave your groove,
Bananas know how to bust a move.
With each rhyme, the forest sings,
In the heart of laughter, happiness springs.

Melodies of the Garden

In the garden, laughter grows,
With fruits that dance, and sunshine glows.
A yellow friend with a silly grin,
Tells jokes to squirrels, let the fun begin!

The petals sway in a jovial tune,
While bees buzz around, they're over the moon.
A gentle breeze brings giggles and cheer,
As daisies chuckle when the end is near.

Lemon pies and pies of cream,
All join in on this funny dream.
A fruit parade, a silly affair,
With laughter echoing, floating in the air.

So here we sway in this joyous land,
With nature's humor, hand in hand.
The garden sings, a whimsical show,
Where smiles abound and good vibes flow.

The Sweetness of Sun-Kissed Bliss

A sunbeam tickles the sweet delight,
As laughter echoes from morning to night.
Gold in the trees, hanging so high,
With giggles aplenty, oh my, oh my!

In the orchard, a slapstick scene,
As fruits get silly, if you know what I mean.
Their peels do wiggle when the wind blows,
And dance round the branches, putting on shows!

A pie of yellow, a custard charm,
With each silly taste, who can do harm?
Under the sun, happiness swells,
In this sweet land, humor dwells.

So gather 'round, let's sing and sway,
In this bright orchard where we love to play.
With laughter ringing, our spirits fly,
In a sun-kissed bliss, beneath the sky.

Bananas in a Gentle Breeze

In the breeze, a yellow cascade,
Wobbling and wobbling, they join the parade.
With hats made of leaves and shoes made of mud,
Our fruity friends roll, it's simply good!

The sun grins down, it's a lively race,
As bananas giggle, keeping up the pace.
Skipping along, they trip on a root,
In this gentle breeze, no need for a suit!

A dance of sweetness, so carefree and bright,
With every twirl, the world feels right.
They break into song, a silly refrain,
In this fruity theme, nothing's mundane!

So come, take part in this playful show,
With bananas twirling, putting on a glow.
In the gentle breeze, let's laugh and spree,
In this cheerful world, happy as can be!

Whirl of the Yellow Glow

A whirl of yellow, spins around,
With giggles rising from underground.
Sprightly fruit in the sunlit air,
Their cheerful antics, beyond compare!

They dance in circles, take a chance,
With every slip, they make us prance.
They spill their secrets, jiggle with pride,
In the warmth of joy, they take us for a ride.

The world's a stage for this fruity play,
With winks and nudges, they steal the day.
A carnival of smiles, laughter does flow,
In the middle of all, the yellow glow.

So let's join hands, twirl and spin,
With our silly friends, let the fun begin.
Laughing together, in cheerful array,
This is our song, come laugh and sway!

Fruitful Dreams

In a jungle vast, where fruits do sway,
Laughter bursts forth in a silly way.
With hats of leaves and shoes of peel,
They dance in rhythm, oh what a reel!

A monkey jigs, with a cheeky grin,
He jokes about the shapes they've been in.
The berries giggle, in colors bright,
While pineapples wobble, what a sight!

All join the feast, with splashes of fun,
Fruit punch spills over, under the sun.
They sing of sweetness, of juicy delight,
Their voices echo, from morning to night.

In dreams they gather, both big and small,
A bonkers party, the best of all.
With fruity hats and friendship's song,
In this silly land, they all belong.

Nature's Sweetest Chime

In orchards lush, where laughter thrives,
Melodies bounce, the fruit's jive.
Pineapples giggle, grapes sway along,
Their peals of joy form nature's song.

Beneath the trees, the apples grin,
Tickling the breeze, a fun-filled spin.
Walnuts crack jokes, oh what a swell,
In the fruit parade, they cast a spell.

Cherries chirp with a wink so sly,
Their laughter floating, oh so high.
Berries bounce, with a happy cheer,
In this fruity realm, there's no fear.

Together they sway, in hues so bright,
Fruits frolic freely, pure delight.
Laughter rings out, so sweet and true,
In this fruitful world, there's fun for you.

Serenade Beneath the Sun

Under the sky, where the sun does smile,
The fruits take stage, in a joyful style.
Bananas swing by, with a silly tune,
While melons roll out, a nutty boon.

Raspberries giggle, in red delight,
Causing off-beats in the warm daylight.
Lemons yell out, with zest and cheer,
Echoes of laughter fill the atmosphere.

Grapefruits bounce, with a jovial shout,
Jams in the making, there's no doubt.
As oranges twist in a funny whirl,
Nature's own dance, watch the fruits twirl.

A serenade plays, on this sunny day,
Where friendships blossom and frolics stay.
With every bite, the humor grows,
In nature's fest, where joy overflows.

Yellow Serenades

In the garden bright, where laughter grows,
Golden fruits tease, with quirky prose.
Bananas prance in a vibrant hue,
Their silly tones sing a tune so true.

Lemon zest bursts, with a playful sound,
While all the fruits gather 'round.
With lollipops glowing in the sun's warm light,
Fruits joke and frolic, oh what a sight!

Mangoes giggle, their sweetness supreme,
Creating a ruckus, living the dream.
From juicy melons to bright pineapple glee,
Each note they sing, a symphony free.

Together they laugh, in joyous parade,
In the funniest dance, they join the brigade.
With yellow serenades, they charm the day,
In this fruity land, come out and play!

Chants of the Canopy

In the leafy green where monkeys swing,
Laughter echoes, oh what joy they bring.
A yellow treat hangs low and bright,
With every bite, a smile takes flight.

Swinging left and swinging right,
Bouncing round in pure delight.
Crack a joke, throw in a pun,
Under the rays of the golden sun.

The squirrels dance, the birds all cheer,
With their goofy moves, they spread the cheer.
A fruity tune plays in the breeze,
Each twist and twirl is sure to please.

So raise a toast to quirky snacks,
With silly hats and jolly quacks.
Nature's banquet, such a sight,
Where humor blooms with pure delight.

Golden Hues and Rhythmic Moves

Golden orbs in the morning light,
Wobble and jiggle, what a sight!
With every beat, they start to sway,
Join the fun, come dance and play.

Giggling ladies in a fruity hue,
Bouncing along, oh how they grew!
Chasing each other in a silly race,
Laughter echoes, filling the space.

Flavors burst like a joyful song,
Sweet and silly, they can't go wrong.
Nature's own little side-show spree,
Who knew that fruit could dance so free?

So grab a friend and start to groove,
Feel the rhythm, find your move.
In this jolly fruit parade, you'll see,
The happiness that comes from glee.

Nature's Edible Ballad

Under the sun, they wave and bow,
Fruity fellows with a cheeky wow.
A strolling band of yellow glee,
Telling tales of their wild spree.

Juggling joy with every turn,
Little giggles, watch them churn.
In the garden, their verses sung,
A harmony that keeps you young.

The ants join in, a tiny crowd,
Marching along, all oh-so-proud.
With every munch, a story shared,
In this charmed grove, none are scared.

So take a taste, and you will find,
A little laughter left behind.
Nature's feast, so bright and bold,
A ballad sweet with stories told.

The Jolly Fruit's Refrain

Round and round, they spin and twirl,
Golden treasures, watch them swirl.
A place where giggles fill the air,
And fruit brings smiles without a care.

With silly hats and wobbly legs,
They dance about, like friendly pegs.
Each move they make, a charming spree,
Joyful moments for you and me.

In every crunch, a chorus sings,
About the fun that laughter brings.
Nature's jesters, bright and spry,
Tickling fancies as they fly.

So join the fun, come take a bite,
In this fruity world, everything's right.
The jolly fruit strums laughter's chord,
In every heart, joy is stored.

Tropical Melodies

In a land where laughter plays,
Fruits wear smiles in sunlit rays.
Coconuts dance, shaking their tops,
While mangoes sing as the fun never stops.

Papayas giggle, ripe and bold,
Chasing shadows, stories told.
Pineapples laugh with spikes so bright,
Joking with limes in the warm twilight.

Bunches of joy hang on each vine,
Swinging gently, sipping sunshine.
With every bite, a giggly cheer,
Tropical tunes ring loud and clear.

Come join the feast, let's all sway,
Fruits in harmony, come what may.
In this realm where humor thrives,
Every taste brings laughter alive.

A Dance of Sunlit Fruits

Underneath the azure skies,
Fruits are frolicking, oh what a prize!
Oranges twirl, wearing their zest,
In this fruity dance, they're simply the best.

Grapes are giggling, rolling so round,
While apples waltz without a sound.
Bananas sway with a twist and spin,
Kicking up fun and mischief within.

Kiwi joins in, a fuzzy delight,
Swinging its seeds with all its might.
Together they jive, beneath the sun's beam,
Creating a laughter-filled, fruity dream.

As the day fades, the laughter stays,
In this tropical world, oh what a craze!
With every melody, joy takes flight,
In the dance of fruits, everything feels right.

Golden Lullaby

In a grove where sunshine sings,
Golden fruits wear joyous rings.
Lullabies float on the evening breeze,
Tickling leaves, it's sure to please.

Mangoes shimmer, soft and sweet,
As they sway to the rhythmic beat.
Lemon laughs with a brightening grin,
Declaring joy is where we begin.

Pineapples snore on their soft green beds,
Dreaming of adventures in lively threads.
Citrus chimes hum a melody slow,
In the golden glow, laughter will grow.

With each note, another cheer,
In this lulling dance of good vibes near.
The night wraps around, soft and light,
As fruity whispers sing through the night.

Whispers in the Grove

In the grove where laughter grows,
Fruits share secrets, everyone knows.
A papaya conspirator, ripe and sly,
Whispers to cherries passing by.

Berries giggle, sprinkled with dew,
Sharing jokes, both silly and true.
Citrus friends with zestful quirks,
Tell tales of sunshine, goofy jerks.

As the breeze rustles, a ticklish tease,
Plums burst out in loud, carefree wheezes.
Avocados blend in, smooth and sly,
Turning every moment into a pie-in-the-sky.

With every rustle, joy does groove,
The orchard thrives, in every move.
Underneath the canopy, laughter flows,
Whispers in the grove, where fun forever glows.

A Song for the Swaying Trees

In the breeze, the leaves do dance,
Each branch sways in a silly prance.
The trunk joins in, a sturdy twist,
Together they laugh, none can resist.

With roots that wiggle, they tease the ground,
A jolly parade, with no one around.
They sing to the sun, oh what a sight,
Their laughter echoes, pure delight!

Squirrels join in with a cheeky cheer,
Punching holes in the air, oh dear!
With acorns falling like little jokes,
They giggle and waltz, those funny folks.

So come join the fun in the swaying trees,
Where giggles flutter on the gentle breeze.
A party of foliage, green and bright,
Making the day feel just right!

Melody of the Orchard Heart

In orchards wide, the fruits delight,
Swinging cheerfully, a joyful sight.
The apples roll, the peaches grin,
Each playful laugh a fruit's soft spin.

The pears chime in with a jolly jingle,
Bouncing and dancing, they twist and mingle.
Beneath the sun, they giggle loud,
A symphony of sweetness, a merry crowd.

Cherries whisper secrets in playful tones,
While strawberries laugh, she won't be alone!
Lemons chuckle, all zesty and bright,
Creating a melody, pure delight.

Join the fun in the orchard's embrace,
Where each fruity burst has its place.
A sweet serenade of laughter and cheer,
In nature's heart, joy makes it clear!

Sunshine's Gentle Tune

Beneath the rays, the daisies sway,
Tickled by warmth on a bright sunny day.
They twirl and spin, with petals so spry,
Singing to birds, as they float by.

The clouds drift in, a fluffy parade,
Making shadows that dance and wade.
Sunshine splashes, a giggly glow,
In this light-hearted, carefree show.

Butterflies flutter like tiny dreams,
Painting the air with their whimsical beams.
Each moment sparkles, alive and sweet,
In this world where laughter and sunlight meet.

Let's join the chorus in fields so wide,
With smiles and laughter, in nature we bide.
A gentle tune that brightens the heart,
In sunshine's embrace, we play our part!

The Joy of Nature's Treat

In the garden blooms a playful scene,
Where blossoms giggle and leaves turn green.
Flowers chuckle in colors so bright,
Bouncing with joy, a whimsical sight.

The bees hum along, a merry refrain,
Dancing in circles through soft spring rain.
They sip on nectar, a sweet little game,
Making a buzz, life's funny name.

Frogs lounge on lilypads, oh what a tease,
Croaking their jokes with the greatest of ease.
With each little splash, a puddle of fun,
Nature's delight under the sun.

So gather around for this treat so fine,
Where laughter flourishes, like sweet summertime.
In nature's own kitchen, joy's served on a plate,
A feast of happiness that's truly first-rate!

Chorus of the Orchard's Heart

In sunlit groves where laughter sways,
Bright yellow friends dance in a haze.
With monkey grins and silly slides,
They sing of joy, where fun abides.

Swinging in trees, oh what a cheer,
Tickling leaves that whisper near.
Their giggles rise like breezy notes,
In this merry band of happy coats.

Each twist and turn, a playful sight,
They bounce and tumble, pure delight.
The orchard echoes, laughter's call,
A fruity ball, the best of all!

So join the fun, don't miss this show,
In yellow hues, let happiness flow.
The orchard's heart, a joyful spark,
With every step, we leave a mark.

A Dance of Yellow Dreams

In a field of gold, they spin around,
Whirling joy where smiles abound.
With every twist, a peel of glee,
A dance of yellow for you and me!

They wear their crowns of sunlit cheer,
Jumping higher, spreading good cheer.
With dance moves bold and jokes set free,
Pure silliness, oh can't you see?

A hop, a skip, they twirl and glide,
In this frolic, all worries hide.
With petals soft and laughter loud,
They weave a magic, proud and unbowed.

So laugh along, let your heart beam,
Join the fun in this yellow dream.
The dance of life, in sunlight's grace,
Find your joy in this silly space.

Songbirds of the Sweet Grove

Oh, songbirds warble with playful cheer,
In the sweet grove, all joys appear.
They flit and flutter in shades of bright,
Singing of snacks and pure delight.

With every note, they tease and play,
Chirping tunes that lighten the day.
From branch to branch, they hop along,
Creating laughter in their song!

Their feathers bright, their spirits free,
Echoing joy like a melody.
In the sweet grove where silliness roams,
They bring sweet smiles, making you feel at home.

So listen close and join the tune,
Under the sun and a cheerful moon.
With every chirp, let spirits rise,
In this groovy place, joy never dies.

Farewell to the Hazy Shade

Under the trees, where shadows play,
The laughter echoes, come what may.
In golden rays, the fun won't cease,
A farewell dance, a joyful feast!

With peels that slip and giggles bright,
The hazy shade bids sweet goodnight.
They roll and tumble, a funny sight,
As stars appear in the tranquil night.

So raise a toast to yellow cheer,
As we bid farewell to the dusky dear.
In memories fond of silly grace,
The orchard whispers, "You'll find your place!"

With every laugh, a treasure made,
In this sweet life, we're never afraid.
So wave goodbye, but never fret,
The fun of today, we won't forget!

Grove's Gentle Harmony

In the grove where fruit can sway,
A yellow smile lights up the day.
With laughter sweet upon the breeze,
The trees all dance with perfect ease.

Fruits wear hats of sunny hue,
Jokes are tossed like morning dew.
A monkey swings to share a grin,
He knows the fun is just begun.

Tickled leaves begin to shake,
Nature sings for giggles' sake.
A rhythm found in every sway,
As joy in fruit takes time to play.

So join the laugh, make merry cheer,
In this grove, there's naught to fear.
With each fruit's chuckle in the air,
Life's a party, everywhere!

Tropical Echoes

Underneath skies bright and wide,
Fruits in laughter, side by side.
From leafy cups, the giggles rise,
Echoes bright like sweet surprise.

Coconuts toss wisecracks near,
While shadows dance, they lend an ear.
Brightly colored, all in tune,
They shake and shimmy 'neath the moon.

The busy breeze joins in the fun,
And tickles toes of everyone.
A bouncy beat, a joyful song,
In this party, we all belong!

So swing along, don't miss the chance,
In the grove, we'll join the dance.
Laughter blooms, it fills the air,
Tropical joy, without a care!

Whimsy in the Canopy

High above, the branches sway,
In bright green robes they laugh and play.
Fruits hang low, like jester hats,
With giggles shared by playful chats.

Squirrels slide in joyous loops,
Dancing under laughing groups.
The swing of vines, a funny sight,
As shadows play, both day and night.

The sunbeams wink, the breeze just sighs,
With every bloom, a fresh surprise.
In this canopy, fun runs free,
A weird and wacky jubilee!

So come and join this fanciful ride,
In the canopy, there's joy inside.
With every chuckle, life becomes bright,
Embrace the whimsy, feel the light!

Verses Beneath the Palm

Beneath the palm, the shadows prance,
As fruits prepare for a funny dance.
Every rustle tells a tale,
Of giggles caught in the sweet, warm gale.

Pineapples wear their spiky crowns,
While lemons tease with goofy frowns.
In colorful hues, they take the stage,
Inviting all to join the page.

With each chuckle and delightful shout,
The fun above keeps spiraling out.
In this realm, let your grin unfold,
For the playful spirit never grows old!

So gather 'round, let laughter soar,
Under palm trees, who could ask for more?
In this fest, we sing with glee,
Life's a party, wild and free!

Lullaby of the Orchard

In the trees where laughter grows,
Fruits wear smiles in sunny rows.
With a wiggle and a dance,
They all join in, a merry chance.

Twilight whispers on the breeze,
A fruity tune among the leaves.
The squirrels giggle, birds take flight,
Sway with me 'neath the moonlight.

Yellow crowns in morning's glow,
Swinging low, they steal the show.
With a squeeze and a juicy squirt,
Nature's gag as laughter flirts.

Now the orchard drifts to sleep,
But dreams of fun, we shall keep.
For in this place of golden cheer,
Tomorrow brings the joy so near.

Serenade of Silken Skins

Gentle ripples of the fair,
Silken skins, beyond compare.
In bright parades, they twirl and spin,
With each chuckle, joy begins.

Climbing high, the monkeys shout,
Peeling layers, swirling about.
A tasty treat, a silly fling,
Watch them pop and joyfully swing.

Jokes aplenty under the sun,
With a wink, we join the fun.
Slipping, sliding, laughter rings,
Life is sweet with fruity flings.

As night descends, the giggles fade,
In leafy dreams, we've serenade.
Tomorrow's sun will bring anew,
The joy of fruits in every hue.

Rhythm of Ripe Fruit

A jolly beat in orchards bright,
Where fruits all bounce in pure delight.
With each jiggle, laughter swells,
Nature sings, and joy compels.

Twirling round with sunny cheer,
Little critters gather near.
In a line, they jump and sway,
Singing tunes of yesterday.

Bananas giggle, apples cheer,
Gather round, come join right here.
In this circle, joy takes flight,
With every bounce, the mood feels right.

When the stars begin to glow,
They dance on air, putting on a show.
In the hush of night's embrace,
The rhythm slows, but hearts still race.

Ballad of the Yellow Delight

Oh sing to me of fruit divine,
The yellow ones, so bright they shine.
In the sun, they frolic free,
Tiny giggles, purest glee.

Joyful bunches hanging near,
Swings of laughter fill the sphere.
With a twist and a playful bounce,
See the critters, watch them pounce.

Every peel, a burst of fun,
Morning rays, a golden run.
In this garden, laughter blooms,
Echoing through all the rooms.

As twilight drapes in soothing tones,
The playful hues create soft moans.
With spirits high, we bid goodnight,
Tomorrow brings delight, so bright.

Tropical Dance of Delight

In the sun, all in line,
Fruits are swaying just fine.
A twist, a turn, what a sight,
Yellow smiles, pure delight.

Lively laughter fills the air,
In every corner, everywhere.
With a jig and a happy cheer,
Everyone's welcome here!

Funky moves of every kind,
Swaying leaves and branches wind.
Join the rhythm, don't be shy,
Underneath the bright blue sky.

When the breeze joins in the fun,
Dancing shadows 'til we're done.
With fruits jiving, oh what a show,
In this grove, the joy will flow.

Whispers in the Green Canopy

Up above, the leaves do sway,
Whispers play, come join the fray.
Fruits are giggling, can't you tell?
In the grove, all is well.

Beneath the shade, we gather round,
With every twist, a joy is found.
A little jig, a little bounce,
From fruit to fruit, we all denounce.

Mirthful echoes, what a sound,
Laughter leaps from ground to ground.
Swinging branches, oh so green,
In this dance, we're all seen.

Join the chatter, join the cheer,
Every voice, we hold dear.
Beneath the canopy so bright,
Sing with glee, till comes the night.

Ode to the Fruit of Joy

Oh fruit so bright, with dress of gold,
In your laughter, stories told.
Bouncing cheer with every peel,
What a joy this dance feels!

Soft and sweet, a tasty bite,
In our hearts, you bring delight.
Rolling smiles, in sunlit glow,
Swinging side to side, we go.

Each moment spent, a treasure true,
With every jig, we celebrate you.
Joyful bounce, a playful fling,
Oh how we love to dance and sing!

In this orchard, we find our place,
With fruits and friends, we fill the space.
Lively laughter fills the air,
To you, dear fruit, we declare!

A Swing Through the Grove

In the grove, a sweet surprise,
Swaying gently 'neath the skies.
Fruits a-dancing, join the fun,
Laughing softly, one by one.

Round and round, we skip and hop,
Never wanting this to stop.
With a wink and a merry grin,
The joy of fruit is where we begin!

Breezes giggle through the leaves,
As the playful spirit weaves.
Time to groove, to swirl around,
With every stomp, the laughter's found!

Let's take a swing, a dance, a whirl,
In this fruit-filled, joyous twirl.
With every move, our hearts expand,
Together, let's make this joyful stand!

Symphony of Sweetness

In a bright yellow coat, they sway and spin,
Hanging on branches, a joyful din.
With laughter and giggles, they dance in the sun,
Sweet little pods, oh, what fun!

A tune made of peels, they wiggle and jive,
Catching the breeze, they're so alive.
With a plop and a squish, they come tumbling down,
Bopping along, always wearing a crown.

With smoothies and splits, they bring us delight,
A chorus of flavors, oh what a sight!
They leap in the air with a playful bounce,
In the land of the sweet, they love to prance.

So gather around, join in the cheer,
For the vibrant show that we hold dear.
Singing with joy, they twist on the vine,
In this symphonic feast, sweet fruits intertwine.

Verses from the Bunch

In a land of bright fruits, a bunch comes alive,
With giggles and grins, they bounce and thrive.
Peeling with laughter, they share tales so grand,
A fruity orchestra, simply unplanned.

Riding the waves of a summer's breeze,
Swinging and swaying, they do as they please.
With each silly wiggle, a new tale they weave,
Creating a rhythm, a song to believe.

The colors of joy, they shine like the sun,
Filled with sweet nectar, oh, such a fun run.
With tinkles and chuckles, their voices entwine,
Each note a reminder of sweet, sunny times.

So come take a seat, don't miss out on the show,
With smiles that spread, like rainbows they glow.
In this happy saga, they leap and they sing,
Together in laughter, the warmth they bring.

A Melody in the Mist

In the twilight garden, where dreams come to play,
The fruits gather round, in a funny display.
With a shimmer of joy, they sway to the tune,
Under the glow of a bright silver moon.

Their skins a soft yellow, so smooth to the touch,
They giggle and wiggle, it tickles so much.
With whispers of sweetness, they cast their delight,
Creating a melody that dances in flight.

In the mist of the morning, they twirl and they leap,
Sharing their secrets, a harvest to keep.
With each happy note, they echo through trees,
A symphonic treat on the whimsical breeze.

So gather your laughter, let joy take the lead,
These funny little fruits plant a joyful seed.
In harmony's glow, they twist and they play,
A melody that brightens the dullest of days.

Sweet Serenade of Summer

On a sunny afternoon, they bask in the light,
With a splash of pure fun, what a delightful sight!
Their laughter erupting, as they dance in the air,
Creating sweet magic, a slice of fair share.

With sugary giggles, they gather in rows,
A friendly parade, where everyone knows.
They bob and they weave, with joy in their core,
Singing their mantra, 'Oh, we want more!'

In a whirl of delight, they merge and collide,
With the jests of each other, they joyfully glide.
Tantalizing taste, they brighten the hour,
In this summer serenade, they bloom like a flower.

So hold out your hands, let the fun be your guide,
As these witty delights take you for a ride.
With each juicy bite, laughter fills the air,
In this sweet serenade, let go of all care.

Whimsical Yellow Ballad

A yellow fruit with a curve so bright,
Hangs on the tree, what a silly sight!
It wiggles and giggles, full of delight,
Swinging in sunshine, oh what a flight!

When folks pass by, they can't help but grin,
Imagining antics, the laughter within.
Peeling away, oh where to begin?
It's love at first bite, just take a spin!

In smoothies, or cakes, it finds its fame,
With each tasty bite, it's always the same.
Bouncing around in its laughter game,
A jolly companion, never to tame!

So here's to the fruit that's a whimsical cheer,
A sassy, sweet friend who draws us all near.
With flavors so bright, let's all give a cheer,
To the jolly yellow, that's always sincere!

Touch of Paradise

In a tropical land where laughter grows,
A fruit like the sun in bright yellow glows.
It dangles from trees and sways with the breeze,
Bringing joy to our hearts, it aims to please.

With each playful slip, it dances around,
In kitchens and lunchboxes, it's always found.
Monkey mischief calls, come join in the fun,
A slippery giggle that's second to none!

In pies and in puddings, it's pure delight,
The taste of a summer, a charming bite.
With friends gathered 'round, we feast and we play,
In a touch of paradise, we savor the day!

So lift up your voices, let's shout out with glee,
For the silly, sweet fruit that's the life of the spree.
It's laughter and sunshine, all wrapped in a peel,
A whimsical treasure—oh, what a meal!

Singing with the Breeze

A yellow delight on a lovely day,
It strums to the rhythm in its playful way.
Breezes are dancing as it sings along,
A fruity ensemble, the world is its song.

With every sweet bite, it swirls in delight,
It tickles the tastebuds, a jubilant fight.
From breakfast to snacks, it steals every show,
This cheerful comedian, in laughter it'd grow!

In smoothies or splits, it reigns supreme,
A fruity adventure, oh what a dream!
Let's gather and share in its supple embrace,
For joy's in the air, it's a fruity race!

So dance with the flavors, let's all spin around,
Join the fun of the glee that's found.
For in every laugh, let its essence be free,
A yellow delight singing with the breeze!

Swaying in Harmony

In the dance of the trees where the laughter flows,
A yellow delight twirls and freely glows.
It sways with the rhythm, a playful tease,
A fruity performer, oh what a breeze!

From monkeying around to slips on the floor,
This fruit shares its giggles, who could ask for more?
In custards and cakes, it finds its own tune,
Creating a melody that brightens the room!

With every sweet moment, it invites us near,
A bundle of joy that banishes fear.
In all of its splendor, it knows how to play,
As we sway in harmony, hip-hip-hooray!

So gather your friends, let the laughter ignite,
For the yellow delight that's a pure bundle of light.
With every bright bite, let's raise up our cheer,
In the swaying embrace of joy throughout the year!

Joys of the Sun-Drenched Realm

In the field where laughter grows,
Fruits abound in sunny rows.
The squirrels dance, the bees take flight,
A fruity feast, what pure delight!

With giggling leaves that sway and play,
And shadows cast in bright array.
The warmth of sun upon the skin,
A golden day, let joy begin!

The Yellow Whisper in the Wind

A secret tickle in the air,
A fruity friend without a care.
He whispers jokes as breezes blow,
With every gust, a cheerful show!

He hides among the leafy trees,
Telling stories with such ease.
Each yellow curve, a playful grin,
A wind-swept dance where giggles spin!

Rhythms of an Abundant Grove

In the grove, a beeping tune,
Where nature hums beneath the moon.
Swinging vines with playful zest,
Invite the critters for a jest!

The fruits jiggle, shake, and bounce,
As silly songs the creatures flounce.
A cacophony of bright delight,
Echoes through the starry night!

Jubilee of Nature's Bounty

A festival under the blazing sun,
Where laughter lives and life is fun.
With every fruit and joyous cheer,
The world spins round, we hold it dear!

Silly hats and dancing shoes,
In this bounty, we cannot lose.
With cheerful hearts, we gather near,
To celebrate, our love sincere!

Chorus of Harvest's Bounty

In fields so bright, the laughter grows,
Where yellow treats dance like prose.
With every peel, a giggle waits,
Nature's jest at the garden gates.

Bananas swing on leafy dreams,
Their cheerful faces burst at the seams.
In playful swings, they bounce around,
Spreading joy where the earth is found.

Rapture of the Gilded Sunrise

As dawn unfolds with a golden grin,
Fruitful whims begin to spin.
The sky hums a silly tune,
To cheer for the harvest, merry as a loon.

Shapes of yellow in morning light,
Twirl with laughter, a comical sight.
Each ripe curve brought forth with flair,
Bringing chuckles through the air.

The Lively Lilt of Nature

A chorus grows from vines that twist,
Under sun's gleam, they persist.
With thickening skins and playful pouts,
They crack jokes and chase out doubts.

Sweetness drips from frolicsome peels,
Nature's humor, it truly reveals.
Giggles echo through the green,
In each little laughter, joy is seen.

Dappled Sunshine's Melody

In the dappled shade where laughter hides,
Bunches swing like wild rides.
With every bite bursting forth delight,
Golden giggles in the bright sunlight.

Poking fun at fruitless frowns,
They parade through sunny towns.
Their jovial spirit takes the stage,
A fruity frolic, they engage.

www.ingramcontent.com/pod-product-compliance
Lightning Source LLC
Chambersburg PA
CBHW060126230426
43661CB00003B/350